Revolutionary Rogues

JOHN ANDRÉ AND BENEDICT ARNOLD

SELENE CASTROVILLA

ILLUSTRATED BY **JOHN O'BRIEN**

CALKINS CREEK
AN IMPRINT OF HIGHLIGHTS
Honesdale, Pennsylvania

For information about permission to
reproduce selections from this book,
please contact permissions@highlights.com.

Calkins Creek
An Imprint of Highlights
815 Church Street
Honesdale, Pennsylvania 18431
Printed in China

ISBN: 978-1-62979-341-2

Library of Congress Control Number: 2016959834

First edition

10 9 8 7 6 5 4 3 2 1

Designed by Barbara Grzeslo
Production by Sue Cole
Titles set in Copperplate Gothic Bold
Text set in Minion Medium
The illustrations are done in pen and
    ink (Rapidograph) and watercolor
    (Dr. Ph. Martin's Hydrus) on
    Strathmore 4-ply Bristol vellum surface.

FOR KENT L. BROWN JR. —SC

FOR TESS —JO'B

"I am perfectly and
tranquil in mind
and prepared for any Fate
to which an honest Zeal
for my Kings Service
may have devoted me."
—*John André*

"Self preservation
is the first principle
of human nature."
—*Benedict Arnold*

MAJOR JOHN ANDRÉ,
bright and well educated, worked closely with General
Sir Henry Clinton, commander in chief of the British army. André
wrote much of Clinton's correspondence. In 1779, Clinton appointed
the twenty-eight-year-old to be adjutant-general and his chief
administrative officer. Soon after, André was also put in charge of
British secret intelligence. Though he had no background in
espionage, he was excited by this new opportunity to serve such
an important role and to prove himself. He longed for glory.

MAJOR GENERAL BENEDICT ARNOLD

was one of America's finest soldiers. The thirty-six-year-old's grit and fervor led to victory at the Battle of Saratoga in 1777. Commander in Chief General George Washington publicly acknowledged Arnold's brilliance and bravery at the battle, but Arnold was denied official credit and passed over for a medal. Reward and recognition were in the U.S. Congress's hands. Arnold had been gravely injured at Saratoga—shot in his leg and maimed. Gone was any further chance for glory *on* the battlefield. He would seek it another way.

MAY 1779
BRITISH HEADQUARTERS, NEW YORK CITY
FOUR YEARS INTO THE WAR

Major John André plopped down in his favorite damask chair, dizzied by the unexpected letter in his hand. John hadn't been in charge of British intelligence for long. He'd been making lists of American officers to solicit, never thinking that one would come to him.

But why would the most heroic of
George Washington's generals agree to treason?
Perhaps Benedict Arnold's new wife played a
part in this. Peggy Shippen Arnold was a British
sympathizer. However, this was not John's
concern. He needed only to seal the deal.
Already, he saw a promotion in his future.

John drew out his quill and a blank sheet. *Yes*, he scrawled. The decision to accept Arnold's offer was simple. The details would be more involved.

Of course, they would need a secret code to communicate. John labored to create one.

Signing the paper "John Anderson"—his new alias—he felt a swell of pride. He relished intrigue! Then John drew another sheet. It was important to report everything to Sir Henry Clinton, his commander.

Finished! All that remained was to wait for Arnold's reply. John beamed as bright as the oil lamps in the room. His job well done! The war had gone on far longer than expected. He would be the one to bring the rebels down.

SEPTEMBER 1780
A TAVERN NEAR ARNOLD'S COMMAND AT WEST POINT, NEW YORK
FIVE YEARS INTO THE WAR

Major General Benedict Arnold sat in dim candlelight in the rear, drinking ale and brewing resentment. He was a hero, with bravery etched in his record and a leg maimed in battle, proof of his sacrifice. Did George Washington appreciate his efforts? No. Blast him.

Benedict's countrymen should have cheered him, rewarded him with gold!

Yes, he was commander of West Point, a key stronghold along New York's Hudson River. But his wife Peggy's standard of living far outranked his salary, and now they had a son. What choice did he have but to carry through with his plan? He was going to hand West Point to the British, along with his three thousand troops.

Benedict scraped his foot across the sawdust-covered wood planks. Silently, he cursed humanity for forcing him into this dark position.

Benedict shuddered at the ugliness of the word *treason*, but
people would be grateful for the end of this long war—and a return
to order. Benedict Arnold would be their hero. Finally, the glory he'd
spent his life seeking *would* be his.

Communications with John André proved long and difficult.
The code was misunderstood, letters were lost, payment negotiations
stalled. Tomorrow they would meet and settle matters. And then,
the attack on West Point could proceed.

Benedict sipped the last of his ale and smirked. George
Washington was making an unscheduled trip to West Point. If his
terms were agreed to quickly, Benedict could also deliver the
American commander in chief.

DEAD OR ALIVE.

SEPTEMBER 1780
NEAR HAVERSTRAW, NEW YORK
17 MILES FROM WEST POINT

John awaited Arnold amidst a forest of fir trees in no-man's-land, territory that belonged to neither the British nor the Americans. But dangerous nevertheless. Americans patrolled the area, scouting for signs of enemy activity on the Hudson River. If they looked tonight, they might spy the British warship *Vulture* anchored in wait for the young officer. His exit was nearby—as long as American cannons didn't fire at the ship!

John forced himself to think past all this danger and suspense—to the taking of West Point! And beyond that: glorious praise and an inevitable promotion!

He was glad for the dark, which covered his uniform. Sir Henry had stressed that wearing a disguise was not an option. Nor was John to take papers from the meeting. If he were caught doing these things, he would be considered a spy—and captured spies were hanged.

PERISH THE THOUGHT OF BEING CAUGHT!

Arnold arrived, and the two soldiers shook hands. They sat on a bed of needles to settle the payment. Finally, the price was agreed upon, and John made a promise: Benedict Arnold would become an officer in the British army should the attack on West Point fail.

BUT THE ATTACK WOULD *NOT FAIL!*

It was late, and they still needed a plan. Arnold proposed they
travel to a home nearby. The ride through the woods seemed endless!

Arnold halted by a shrub to talk to someone. A secret code must have been passed. John swallowed hard, trying to dissolve the lump that had formed in his throat. They'd crossed American lines!

He swallowed again. All he had to do was get through this night—and glory would be his.

SHORTLY AFTER
INSIDE THE HOME OF JOSHUA HETT SMITH

Hours passed, and day broke. John looked out the window toward the Hudson River and saw that the *Vulture* was still there! The lump in his throat melted. This ordeal was almost finished. After breakfast, he would journey back to the river—and the *Vulture*.

A thunderous blast shook the walls. John rushed to the window: the *Vulture* was fleeing American fire! Knees wobbling, John clutched the sill. With at least twenty miles between him and British territory and the only way out on foot, John realized the deep trouble he was in. How ever would he return to New York?

The lump in his throat was back.

STILL INSIDE
SMITH'S HOUSE

Benedict stared at the quivering André with contempt. Coward! A fine head of intelligence *he* was.

No time for drama—Benedict had been absent from headquarters too long. He settled things quickly: Smith would guide André back into neutral territory. From there, he would be fine alone. André would wear a tattered jacket and round beaver hat and stow Arnold's plans for West Point in his boot.

André balked: he had orders to remain in uniform and carry nothing.

Arnold insisted: André *would* wear the disguise. How far did he hope to get in a British uniform? And he *would also* carry the plans—*proof* of Arnold's hard work.

André could not win the fight. He shed his uniform and stuffed the papers in his boot.

Well done, Benedict told him. Now, if he'd just stop shaking!

THE FOLLOWING DAY
NO-MAN'S-LAND NEAR
TARRYTOWN, NEW YORK

John was alone, having made it through enemy lines.

The worst was over; the weather, pleasant. John breathed in the air and admired the colorful leaves.

At the end of a bridge, three horsemen appeared, blocking his path.

They were grimy, dressed in military cast-off clothes much like his disguise.

Perhaps if he just nodded and gave a slight smile, they would let him pass. He dared not speak, least they detect his British accent.

But the men remained stone-faced and didn't budge. The middle one raised a musket.

John had no time to panic before he was ordered from his horse. Strip! they commanded him. Starting with his boots.

John could only obey. When the plans for West Point tumbled out, the thieves realized: they'd stumbled on a spy!

John pleaded: his commander would pay well for his freedom, but the ruffians banked on the Americans rewarding them more.

Ordered back on his horse, John was led toward American soil. The trees looked muddy brown now, and the crisp air proved harder to breathe.

Smith reported back to Benedict during supper. All was well. "John Anderson" was on his way home.

THE SAME EVENING
AN AMERICAN OUTPOST IN SOUTH SALEM, NEW YORK

John paced the perimeter of his cell with the precise steps of a gentleman. Even as he panicked, his breeding didn't falter. The clicking rhythm of his boots sounded on the floorboards.

There was no way out now. The plans he'd carried were on their way to General Washington.

Also on its way was a letter to West Point's commander, Benedict Arnold, informing him of John's capture in Arnold's territory.

John knew Arnold would not try to save him.

The truth was John's only option. Requesting pen and paper, John
scrawled a letter confessing his identity and begging mercy.
His fate rested in the heart of George Washington.

THE FOLLOWING MORNING
ARNOLD'S HEADQUARTERS

Benedict nearly choked on his eggs when the note about André arrived. Jumping to his feet, he scattered silverware in a scrambled panic. He bellowed orders to his servants: Saddle my horse! Tell the barge crew to stand by!

Then he climbed the stairs to Peggy. He *had* to bid her good-bye.

Making haste back down the creaking steps, Benedict banged out the front door. His horse was ready—he could make it!

From up the road came clamoring hooves: Washington with his men.
Benedict raced his steed down the steep slope to the river. At the
water's edge, he dismounted and boarded his barge. Finding the *Vulture*
was his only hope. He bayed at his crew: paddle—*fast!*

Eighteen miles out, he spotted the British ship. Tying a white handkerchief to his cane, Benedict directed his men to approach. The men hesitated, but he told them to fear not: he carried a message from Washington.

The crew delivered their commander to the *Vulture*. Benedict invited them on board, then revealed the truth. He promised his men promotions if they switched sides and joined the British army. But the men refused to turn traitor, as Benedict Arnold clearly was. Offended, Benedict declared them prisoners to be locked inside the *Vulture*'s hold!

Benedict wrote a letter to Washington, insisting he'd acted out of love for his country. He appealed: protect Peggy, who was as good and as innocent as an angel. He also excused Joshua Hett Smith, who knew nothing of the plot. There was no mention of John André.

The sealed note was dispatched with a rowboat crew, and the *Vulture* set course for New York.

OCTOBER 1780
TAPPAN, NEW YORK

John was about to die. But there would be no tears. He would leave this world with courage. If he couldn't have glory, he could at least be brave.

The trial had been quick; Washington, merciless. In exchange for John, Sir Henry had offered every American prisoner he held. Washington wanted only one person: Benedict Arnold. Alas, that could not be. Arnold had secured protection with the British when he'd negotiated his deal.

It was time. Escorted from his cell, John wore his uniform. Sir Henry had sent it.

Outside, he squinted in the harsh light. People lined the street and watched him climb the steep hill. At the top, he stepped up to the gallows with his head held high. He asked his audience to bear witness: "I meet my fate like a brave man."

John reached for the noose, placed it around his neck, and drew the knot close. The weight of the rope, the bristles—these were the last things he'd feel.

A whip cracked. A jolt as the horses bolted with the wagon under him.

THEN, DARKNESS.

OCTOBER 1780
BRITISH HEADQUARTERS, NEW YORK

Benedict sat in André's chair, surrounded by André's belongings. There was no eluding the hanged man. André was the toast of the town, mourned by the British army and martyred for his gallant sacrifice.

Benedict had escaped, but to what? Never again would he be trusted. A traitor once was a traitor always. Gone was his last chance for glory. Somehow André's death had secured this—a bolt tightening a chain. And although Benedict felt something in André's death, he couldn't call it sorrow. No, it was jealousy. André had taken his role.

BENEDICT ARNOLD WOULD NEVER BE CALLED VALIANT, BUT JOHN ANDRÉ FOREVER WOULD.

AFTERMATH

When he reached New York City, Benedict Arnold was commissioned into the British army as a brigadier general. General Arnold led raids in Virginia and Connecticut, but Sir Henry Clinton made sure Arnold didn't act alone. He was always accompanied by other generals.

George Washington honored Benedict's plea to spare his wife. Peggy and her son, Edward, headed to New York where the British were still headquartered and Benedict was based.

Arnold remained in service until the war drew to a close. In December 1781, Benedict, Peggy, Edward, and their second son, James, sailed to England.

George Washington had little to say about the man who betrayed him. When asked how he thought Arnold might feel after André's hanging, Washington replied: "He wants feeling."

Of André, Washington said, "He was more unfortunate than criminal." He added later that André was "an accomplished man and gallant officer."

Major Benjamin Tallmadge, one of Washington's most trusted soldiers, talked to André before his death and wrote: "For the few days of intimate intercourse I had with him, . . . I became so deeply attached to Major Andre, that I can remember no instance where my affections were so fully absorbed in any man. When I saw him swinging under the gibbet, it seemed for a time as if I could not support it. All the spectators seemed to be overwhelmed by the affecting spectacle, and many were suffused in tears. There did not appear to be one hardened or indifferent spectator in all the multitude."

André was buried at the sight where he was hanged, in Tappan, New York. Two years later, King George III commissioned and paid for a monument to André in Westminster Abbey, London, England, one of the world's great churches. Forty-one years after his hanging, the body of John André was exhumed and returned to England. He was laid to rest with honors at Westminster Abbey, by his monument.

On October 2, 1879—ninety-nine years after André was hanged—a stone monument was erected in Tappan in his memory. Inscribed on it is a quotation, in Latin, from a work by the poet Virgil: *Sunt lacrimae rerum et mentem mortalia tangunt*, meaning, "These are the tears of things, and our mortality cuts to the heart."

Suffering from asthma, gout, and his never-ending inner torment, Arnold died in bed at age sixty in London. He had lived away from the United States for nearly twenty years.

Peggy died three years later, from cancer.

Peggy and Benedict had seven children. At the time of her death, five remained. Their four sons all served in the British military.

Benedict, Peggy, and their daughter Sophia are buried in a crypt at St. Mary's Church Battersea in London. Benedict was not given military honors. There was little to commemorate him. But in 1976, a private donor and Arnold enthusiast paid for a stained-glass church window at St. Mary's in his honor. Benedict is pictured surrounded by American and British flags.

The American army denied Benedict Arnold his name as a hero. At the site of the Battle of Saratoga, the inscription on a monument reads: "In Memory of the 'most brilliant soldier' of the Continental Army . . ."

Inside a small chapel at West Point are plaques dedicated to generals of the American Revolution. Arnold's plaque bears only his rank and birth year.

The world denied Benedict Arnold his name.

It wasn't long before it came to mean "traitor."

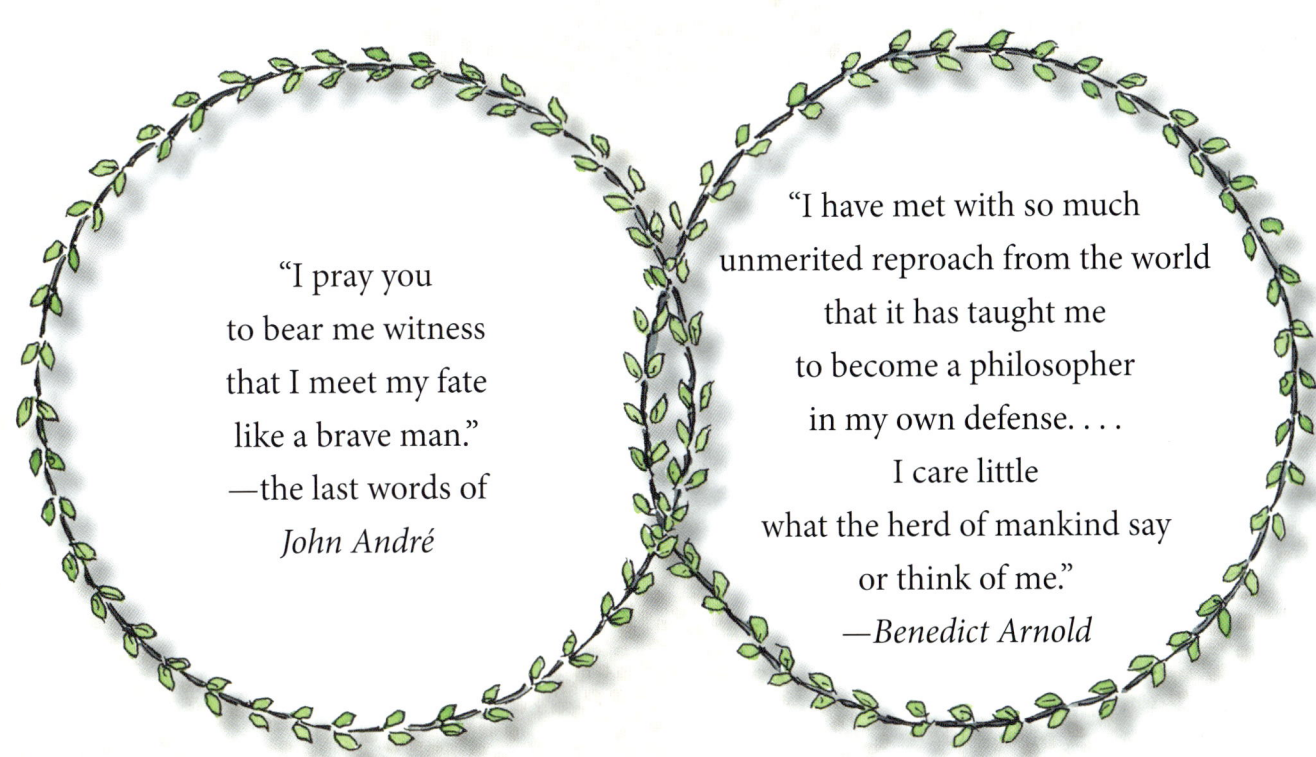

"I pray you
to bear me witness
that I meet my fate
like a brave man."
—the last words of
John André

"I have met with so much
unmerited reproach from the world
that it has taught me
to become a philosopher
in my own defense. . . .
I care little
what the herd of mankind say
or think of me."
—*Benedict Arnold*

THE LIFE OF
JOHN ANDRÉ

1750 MAY 2—Born in London, England.

1770 Enters the British army.

1774 Joins his regiment in Canada as a lieutenant.

1775 Captured at Canada's Fort Saint-Jean by invading Americans; held prisoner in Lancaster, Pennsylvania.

1776 Released in a prisoner exchange.

1777 SEPTEMBER—The Americans flee Philadelphia. André, now a captain, moves into Benjamin Franklin's abandoned house. He befriends Margaret (Peggy) Shippen, seventeen-year-old daughter of loyalist Edward Shippen.

1778 JUNE—The British evacuate Philadelphia. André accompanies Sir Henry Clinton to New York and is promoted to major. He is also appointed deputy adjutant-general of the British army in America.

1779 Becomes adjutant-general of the British army in America and head of British secret intelligence; receives an offer of treason from Benedict Arnold.

1780 SEPTEMBER—André sails up the Hudson River on the British warship *Vulture* to meet Arnold in the woods below Stony Point. They proceed to West Haverstraw, New York, to finish negotiations. André is captured in Tarrytown, New York, while trying to return to British territory and is held at the Mabie Inn during his trial at the Reformed Church of Tappan.
OCTOBER—Found guilty of spying, André is hanged and buried at that spot.

1782 A monument to André is erected in Westminster Abbey, London, England.

1821 André's body is exhumed and sent to England and laid to rest with honors at Westminster Abbey.

1879 On the ninety-ninth anniversary of his death, a monument to André is placed on the site of his hanging in Tappan, New York.

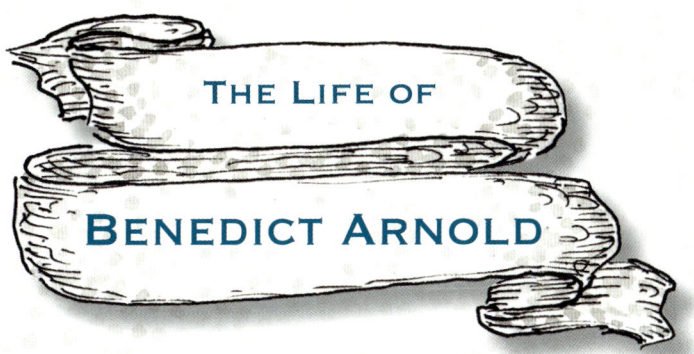

THE LIFE OF

BENEDICT ARNOLD

1741 JANUARY 14—Born in Norwich, Connecticut.

1755 Yearns to join the militia in service against the French; his mother denies permission.

1757 Joins the militia but sees no action; returns home with his company after thirteen days.

1767 Marries Margaret Mansfield; they will have three sons: Benedict, Richard, and Henry.

1775 In the early stirrings of the Revolutionary War, Arnold joins Connecticut's militia as a captain. He is soon promoted to colonel and helps capture British Fort Ticonderoga in New York. On his way home, he receives the news that his wife has died. His sister, Hannah, becomes caretaker of his children. Arnold becomes a colonel in the Continental army. He participates in an unsuccessful attack on Quebec, Canada, where his left leg is severely but not permanently injured. He is promoted to brigadier general.

1777 Fights valiantly to defeat the British at Saratoga. His left leg is again injured. Amputation is recommended, but Arnold refuses. The leg is crudely set and, when it heals, is two inches shorter than his right leg.

1778 Returns to the army after months of recovery. He is given the rank of major general and takes an oath of allegiance at Valley Forge, Pennsylvania. When the British withdraw from Philadelphia, George Washington gives Arnold command of the city. Arnold meets and courts loyalist Peggy Shippen.

1779 APRIL—Marries Peggy Shippen. **MAY**—Contacts John André in New York to offer his services to the British.

1780 Arnold and André meet. When Arnold learns of André's capture, he flees to the safety of the British warship *Vulture*. In New York, Arnold is appointed a British brigadier general. His wife and son Edward join him. He heads south to raid Richmond, Virginia.

1781 Relieved of duty in Virginia, Arnold leads raids in Connecticut. Peggy gives birth to a second son. When news of the British loss at Yorktown reaches Arnold, he and his family sail to England.

1784 Suffers with his wife the loss of two infants: Margaret, born in 1783, and George, born in 1784.

1785 A second daughter, Sophia, is born.

1787 Peggy delivers a fourth son, George.

1794 William, the Arnolds' last child, is born.

1801 JUNE 14—Dies at age sixty.

NEW YORK

ANDRE MONUMENT
42 Andre Hill
Tappan

This granite monument marks the spot where John André was hanged in 1780. It stands on a 20-foot-by-20-foot plot, surrounded by a wrought-iron fence.

DEWINT HOUSE
20 Livingston Avenue
Tappan
dewinthouse.com

George Washington headquartered here several times: during John André's trial, earlier in 1780, and twice in 1783.

MORRIS-JUMEL MANSION
65 Jumel Terrace
New York City
morrisjumel.org

Known as Mount Morris during the Revolutionary War, Manhattan's oldest house served as Sir Henry Clinton's headquarters during the British occupation of New York. Before that, George Washington headquartered here. The 130-acre hilltop property afforded views in every direction, making it strategically desirable.

OLD '76 HOUSE
110 Main Street
Tappan
76house.com

During his trial, John André was confined here, when it was known as Mabie's Tavern. It is one of America's oldest taverns and a national landmark. Today, families can dine here and see the room where André spent his last days.

Every October 2, the Tappantown Historical Society hosts an "Andre Walk" for local schoolchildren. It begins in the Old '76 House and follows André's steps to his execution on Andre Hill.

SARATOGA NATIONAL HISTORICAL PARK
648 Route 32
Stillwater
nps.gov/sara/index.htm

Visit the site where the Americans won a critical battle against the British. Benedict Arnold was vital to this win and suffered a crippling leg wound. Boot Monument, which depicts the spurs and stars of a major general, stands on the spot where Arnold was shot, though his name is not mentioned. The Saratoga Monument, a 155-foot stone obelisk, commemorates the Americans' victory. Four compartments are built into the monument. Three hold statues of officers who were critical in the fight. The fourth—where Benedict Arnold would have been honored—is empty.

TAPPAN REFORMED CHURCH
32 Old Tappan Road
Tappan

Site of John André's trial. (The original building is no longer there.)

WEST POINT
Main Street
Highland Falls
westpoint.edu

The key fort Benedict Arnold conspired to hand over to the British is now the United States Military Academy at West Point, a renowned and distinguished college and training facility for the U.S. Army. Guided tours are available.

LONDON, ENGLAND

ST. MARY'S CHURCH BATTERSEA
Battersea Church Road
stmarysbattersea.org.uk

Benedict, Peggy, and Sophia Arnold are buried here. One of the church's four modern stained-glass windows is dedicated to Arnold.

WESTMINSTER ABBEY
20 Deans Yard
westminster-abbey.org

Founded in 960, this world-famous church is the resting place of royalty and prominent people in British history. John André's remains are located in Hero's Corner, by a marble monument. All coronations have taken place at the church since 1066. Prince William and Catherine Middleton were married there in 2011.

---

*Websites active at time of publication

BIBLIOGRAPHY*

All quotations used in the book can be found in the following sources marked with an asterisk (*).

PAPERS (PRIMARY SOURCES)

George Washington Papers, Revolutionary War Series (1775–1783), at the Library of Congress. Manuscript Division, Library of Congress.

*Henry Clinton Papers, William L. Clements Library, University of Michigan.

Thomas Jefferson Papers, Vols. 2–4, Library of Congress.

NEWSPAPERS (Primary Sources)
Pennsylvania Gazette.
Rivington's New York Loyal Gazette.
Royal Gazette.

BOOKS

Abbatt, William. *The Crisis of the Revolution: Being the Story of Arnold and André.* New York: Empire State Society, Sons of the American Revolution, 1899.

Alden, John R. *George Washington: A Biography.* Baton Rouge: Louisiana State University Press, 1984.

André, John. *Major André's Journal.* Tarrytown, NY: William Abbatt, 1930.

Bakeless, John. *Turncoats, Traitors, and Heroes.* Philadelphia: J. B. Lippincott, 1959.

Bakeless, John, and Katherine Bakeless. *Spies of the Revolution.* Philadelphia: J. B. Lippincott, 1962.

Chase, P. D., F. E. Grizzard Jr., D. R. Hoth, E. G. Lengel, et al., eds. *The Papers of George Washington.* Revolutionary War Series. 20 vols. Charlottesville: University Press of Virginia, 1985–2010.

Ferling, John E. *The First of Men: A Life of George Washington.* Knoxville: University of Tennessee Press, 1988.

Fitzpatrick, John C., ed. *The Diaries of George Washington, 1748–1799.* Vol. 2, 1771–1785; vol. 4, 1789–1799. Boston: Houghton Mifflin, 1925.

Flexner, James Thomas. *George Washington in the American Revolution, 1775–1783.* Boston: Little, Brown, 1968.

*———. *The Traitor and the Spy: Benedict Arnold and John André.* Boston: Harcourt, Brace, 1953.

———. *Washington: The Indispensable Man.* Boston: Little, Brown, 1974.

Force, Peter, ed. *American Archives.* 4th and 5th ser. Washington, DC, 1848–1853.

Ford, Corey. *A Peculiar Service.* Boston: Little, Brown, 1965.

Freeman, Douglas Southall. *George Washington: A Biography.* Vol. 5, *Victory with the Help of France.* New York: Charles Scribner's Sons, 1952.

Fritz, Jean. *Traitor: The Case of Benedict Arnold.* New York: Puffin Books, 1981.

Graydon, Alexander. *Memoirs of His Own Time: With Reminiscences of the Men and Events of the Revolution.* Edited by John Stockton Littell. Philadelphia: Lindsay and Blakiston, 1846.

Groh, Lynn. *The Culper Spy Ring.* Philadelphia: Westminster Press, 1969.

Hagman, Harlan L. *Nathan Hale and John André: Reluctant Heroes of the American Revolution.* Interlaken, NY: Empire State Books, 1992.

Harper's New Monthly Magazine. Vol. 52, December 1875–May 1876. Google Books.

Hatch, Robert McConnell. *Major John André: A Gallant in Spy's Clothing.* Boston: Houghton Mifflin, 1986.

*Irving, Washington. *The Life of George Washington.* Vol. 3. New York: G. P. Putnam, 1856.

Jackson, Donald, and Dorothy Twohig, eds. *The Diaries of George Washington.* Charlottesville: University of Virginia Press, 1976.

Johnston, Henry P., ed. *The Correspondence and Public Papers of John Jay.* New York: G. P. Putnam's Sons, 1890–1893.

---

* *Websites active at time of publication*

Kinnaird, Clark. *George Washington: The Pictorial Biography*. New York: Hastings House, 1967.

Morpurgo, J. E. *Treason at West Point: The Arnold-André Conspiracy*. New York: Mason/Charter, 1975.

Newsday. Long Island: Our Story. New York: *Newsday*, 1998.

Old, Wendie C. *George Washington*. Springfield, NJ: Enslow Publishers, 1997.

Pennypacker, Morton. *General Washington's Spies on Long Island and in New York*. Brooklyn, NY: Long Island Historical Society, 1939.

———. *The Two Spies*. Boston: Houghton Mifflin, 1930.

Proceedings of a General Court Martial for the Trial of Major General Arnold. New York: privately printed, 1865. Internet Archive. archive.org/details/proceedingsagen00arnogoog.

Sargent, Winthrop. *Life and Career of Major John André*. New York: Garrett Press, 1969.

Scharf, J. Thomas. *History of Westchester County, New York*. Vol. 2. Philadelphia: L. E. Preston, 1886.

Simcoe, John Graves. *A Journal of the Operations of the Queen's Rangers*. New York: *New York Times*, 1968. Reprint of the 1844 edition published as *Simcoe's Military Journal*.

Smith, Joshua Hett. *An Authentic Narrative of the Causes Which Led to the Death of Major André*. London: Mathews and Leigh, 1808.

Sparks, Jared. *The Life and Treason of Benedict Arnold*. New York: Harper Brothers, 1872.

*Tallmadge, Benjamin. *Memoir of Colonel Benjamin Tallmadge*. New York: Thomas Holman, 1858.

*Thacher, James. *Military Journal of the American Revolution: From the Commencement to the Disbanding of the American Army*. Hartford, CT: Hurlbut, Williams, 1862.

Van Doren, Carl. *Secret History of the American Revolution*. New York: Viking Press, 1941.

Walsh, John Evangelist. *The Execution of Major André*. New York: Palgrave, 2001.

ADDITIONAL SOURCES
UNITED STATES
City Tavern, Philadelphia, Pennsylvania.
David Library of the American Revolution, Washington Crossing, Pennsylvania.
The DeWint House, Tappan, New York (Washington's headquarters).
Fraunces Tavern Museum, New York, New York.
The Old '76 House, Tappan, New York.
The Oyster Bay Historical Society, Oyster Bay, New York.
Raynham Hall Museum, Oyster Bay, New York.
Tappantown Historical Society, Tappan, New York.
Three Village Historical Society, Setauket, New York.
Washington's Headquarters Museum, Morristown, New Jersey.

ENGLAND
British Library, London.
Fusilier Museum, London; independently operated within the Tower of London. (John André was a member of the Royal Welch Fusiliers, now a part of the Royal Regiment of Fusiliers.)
National Army Museum, London.
Somerset House, London.
Westminster Abbey, London.

ACKNOWLEDGMENTS
Thank you to my generous and meticulous experts:
Mary V. Thompson, research historian
    Fred W. Smith National Library for the Study of George Washington
    Mount Vernon, Virginia

Andrew C. Batten, former executive director of Fraunces Tavern Museum, New York City, and Raynham Hall Museum, Oyster Bay, New York, and Revolutionary War educator, lecturer, and consultant

Michael J. F. Sheehan, senior historian
    Stony Point Battlefield State Historic Site
    New York State Office of Parks, Recreation and Historic Preservation

Thanks also to my research assistant, Pascale Laforest.

—SC